Florence Nightingale

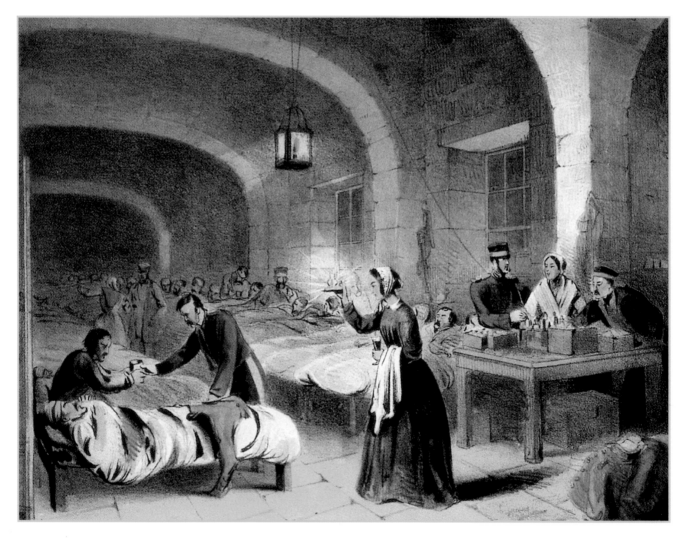

Liz Gogerly

First published in 2007 by Wayland

Copyright © Wayland 2007

Wayland
338 Euston Road
London NW1 3BH

Wayland Australia
Level 17/207 Kent Street
Sydney, NSW 2000

Editor: Victoria Brooker
Designer: Jane Stanley

British Library Cataloguing in Publication Data

Gogerly, Liz
   Who was Florence Nightingale?
   1. Nightingale, Florence, 1820-1910 - Juvenile literature
   2. Nurses - England - Biography - Juvenile literature
   3. Crimean War, 1853-1856 - Women - Juvenile literature
   I. Title
   610.7'3'092

ISBN 978 0 7502 5191 4

Printed in China

Wayland is a division of Hachette Children's Books, a Hachette Livre UK Company.

For permission to reproduce the following pictures, the author and publisher would like
to thank: Mary Evans Picture Library: 18; Getty Images (Hulton Archive): 7, 12, 19;
Library of Congress, USA: 15; © Massimo Listri/Corbis: 6; Werner Otto/Alamy Images:
11; Pictorial Press/Alamy Images: 16; Science Museum/Science & Society Picture Library:
17; Science Museum Pictorial/ Science & Society Picture Library: 5; © Time & Life
Pictures/Getty Images: 4, Cover; Topham Picturepoint/TopFoto.co.uk: 8, 13, 21; Wellcome
Library, London: 10, 14, 20; World History Archive/Alamy Images: 9

Contents

Words in **bold** can be found in the glossary.

Who was Florence Nightingale?

Florence Nightingale was a famous nurse. She was born in 1820. Queen Victoria came to the throne in 1837. So we call the time that Florence worked as a nurse the **Victorian age.**

Florence Nightingale in 1855. This photograph was taken soon after she returned from nursing sick soldiers in Turkey.

At the beginning of the Victorian age nurses were not trained properly. Hospitals were often dirty and badly **organised**. Florence worked to change all this.

IT'S TRUE!

Victorian hospitals were filthy, stinky places. Lots of people died in Victorian hospitals rather than get better.

In Victorian times hospitals were crowded and dirty. This made diseases and germs spread more quickly.

Childhood days

Florence Nightingale was born on 12 May 1820 in Italy while her parents were on holiday. She came from a rich English family. They had large homes in Derbyshire and Hampshire.

A painting of the Italian city of Florence as it looked in Victorian times. Florence's parents named her after the place she was born.

Young Florence was raised to be a lady. Her father gave her lessons at home. Florence was a happy, clever child. Like all Victorian ladies, she was expected to get married one day.

Places to Visit

Claydon House in Buckinghamshire. Florence often visited here as a child. Today, it looks like it did in Victorian times.

A photograph of Embley Park. This was one of the homes where Florence lived as a child.

A call from God

One day Florence was walking in the garden at Embley Park. She thought she heard God call to her. He told her to help other people. At the time Florence was only sixteen. She didn't know what she should do. She began visiting sick people in the villages near her home.

A painting of Florence with her sister Parthenope. Florence is sitting and sewing.

When Florence was nineteen she turned down an offer of marriage. Her parents sent her away to Europe. They hoped a holiday would help change her mind. While she was away Florence decided that she wanted to become a nurse.

IT'S TRUE!

Victorian ladies were not expected to have a **career**. Their job was to look after their home and family.

The poet and politician, Richard Monckton Milnes, was in love with Florence. He asked her to marry him many times but she always turned him down.

Learning to be a nurse

Florence's parents were angry that she wanted to become a nurse. This was not a job for a lady. The family told Florence she could not be a nurse. They would not give her the money she needed. Sometimes her mother and sister did not talk to her.

THE NURSE.

This drawing of an untrained Victorian nurse shows that people often thought nurses were impatient and uncaring.

In 1850 Florence visited a hospital in Germany. It was clean and well **organised**. When she got home Florence's parents finally let her try nursing. The next year she went back to Germany to begin **training**.

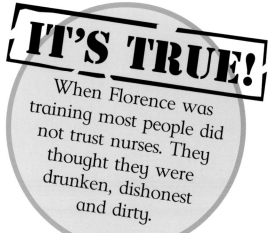

The Institution of Kaiserswerth in Germany as it looks today. This is where Florence trained as a nurse.

A terrible war

Florence was made the **manager** of a woman's hospital in London in 1853. Soon, she was making changes to the way the hospital was run. She cut costs. She tried to make sure there was good food to eat. Florence felt truly happy.

This photograph of Florence was taken in 1854.

In 1854 the **Crimean War** started in Turkey. Florence read about the war in the newspaper. She was upset about the wounded soldiers. Florence wanted to help them.

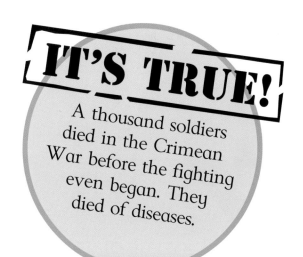

British troops at the Battle of Alma during the Crimean War in 1854.

Florence helps the soldiers

In October 1854 the **government** asked Florence to help the soldiers. Shortly after, she left London with 38 nurses. They went to the army hospital at Scutari, in Turkey.

Florence at the military hospital in Scutari. Florence and the nurses cleaned the hospital and cooked food for the soldiers.

Scutari was worse than Florence imagined. The hospital was filthy and often flooded. Rats and fleas were everywhere. Thousands of ill soldiers filled the hospital. There were not enough beds, bandages, clean sheets or good food for the poor men.

IT'S TRUE!

Photography was a new invention in Victorian times. The **Crimean War** was the first war ever to be photographed.

An early photograph of British soldiers at the Crimea.

The 'Lady with the Lamp'

Florence was kind and talked to her patients. Sometimes she wrote letters home for them. At night she walked along the long lines of beds to check the soldiers. The men called her the 'Lady with the Lamp'.

Florence on the wards at Scutari with her lamp.
She was often on her feet for twenty hours a day.

Florence worked hard but still thousands of men died from disease. Florence nearly died from fever herself. People at home read about Florence in the newspapers. She became famous for her good work.

Places to Visit

You can see the type of lamp that Florence possibly carried at Scutari at the Florence Nightingale Museum in London. There are paintings, letters and many other things that belonged to her there too.

Florence wore these leather slippers while she worked in the hospital at Scutari.

A school for nurses

Florence returned to England in 1857. At Scutari, Florence had learned how disease spread quickly in dirty places. Now she wanted to improve all army hospitals. She worked with the **government** to change the way these hospitals were run.

A sketch of Florence made after the **Crimean war**.

Florence also wanted to start a school for **training** nurses. In 1860 the Nightingale Training School at St Thomas' Hospital in London was opened. The same year Florence wrote a book called *Notes on Nursing*. All her hard work helped to make nursing a better job.

IT'S TRUE!

Nurses who trained at the Nightingale Training School ended up working at hospitals all around the world.

Florence in 1886 with a group of trainee nurses. When the nurses finished training Florence invited them for tea.

A national hero

At Christmas 1861 Florence nearly died from a mystery illness. For years she couldn't walk. This did not stop her from working. She wrote books about **health care** and helped to **design** new hospitals.

In the final years of her life there was always a nurse at Florence's bedside.

As Florence got older she had to stay in bed all the time. Near the end of her life she went blind and could not write. But her good work was never forgotten. In 1907, King Edward VII gave her the **Order of Merit**. She died in 1910 at the age of ninety.

Places to Visit

You can find Florence's grave at St Margaret's Church, East Wellow in Hampshire. The words on her grave are very simple. They read: F. N. Born 1820 Died 1910.

A statue of Florence stands outside St. Thomas' Hospital in London.

Timeline

May 1820	Florence born in Florence, Italy
1837	Florence hears a 'call from God' to help other people
1847	Florence travels to Europe and decides to become a nurse
1850	Florence travels to Egypt and Europe. She makes her first visit to the German hospital, the Institution of Kaiserswerth
1851	Florence returns to the Institution of Kaiserswerth in Germany to begin training as a nurse
1853	Florence becomes manager of a hospital in London
September 1854	The Crimean War begins
October 1854	Florence leaves London for Scutari with 38 nurses
May 1855	Florence is seriously ill with fever and nearly dies
1856	The Crimean War ends
	Florence returns to England
October 1859	Florence writes *Notes on Hospitals*
January 1860	Florence writes *Notes on Nursing*
June 1860	The Nightingale Training School for nurses is opened at St Thomas' Hospital in London
1861	Florence is seriously ill and nearly dies
1902	Florence goes blind and can no longer work
1907	Florence is given the Order of Merit by King Edward VII
August 1910	Florence dies at home in London

Glossary

career the different jobs that a person has during their working life

Crimean War the war in the Crimea that lasted from 1854 to 1856. It was between Russia on one side and England, France, Turkey and Sardinia on the other side

design to make drawings and decide how something should be built or made

government the people who make decisions about how a country should be run

health care the care of the sick by doctors and nurses

manager the person who is in charge of a place where people work

Order of Merit the award is given by the king or queen to people who have achieved something outstanding. Florence Nightingale was the first woman to be admitted for her good works

organised to have arranged things neatly and in order

train/trained/training to learn how to do something properly at a school or college. Florence Nightingale trained how to be a nurse

Victorian age the era in which Queen Victoria was on the throne. This lasted from 1837 to 1901

Further information

Books:

Beginning History: The Life of Florence Nightingale by Liz Gogerly (Wayland, 2003)

Who Was: Florence Nightingale the Lady with the Lamp by Charlotte Moore (Short Books, 2004)

Websites

http://www.bbc.co.uk/schools/famouspeople/standard/nightingale/index.shtml#focus

A colourful website about the life of Florence Nightingale. There is also a quiz for you to do.

http://tlfe.org.uk/clicker/flashhistoryks1/florence.swf

A clear and simple website which tells the story of Florence Nightingale's life. There are excellent pictures and paintings for you to see too.

Index